Sons and Daughters of the Light

W9-AZJ-077

A Pastoral Plan for Ministry with Young Adults

In November 1993 the general membership of the National Conference of Catholic Bishops authorized the Bishops' Committee on the Laity to develop a national plan for pastoral ministry to and with young adults. After wide consultation with dioceses, national organizations, and young adults themselves, the Committee on the Laity submitted the final draft to the plenary assembly of the National Conference of Catholic Bishops. *Sons and Daughters of the Light: A Pastoral Plan for Ministry with Young Adults* was approved on November 12, 1996, and is hereby authorized for publication by the undersigned.

Monsignor Dennis M. Schnurr
General Secretary
NCCB/USCC

ISBN 1-57455-127-2

First Printing, January 1997
Third Printing, September 1999

Scriptural excerpts from *The New American Bible* used with permission of the copyright holder, Confraternity of Christian Doctrine, copyright © 1970, 1986, 1991. All rights reserved.

Copyright © 1996, United States Catholic Conference, Inc., Washington, D.C. All rights reserved. No part of this work may be reproduced or transmitted in any form or by any means, electronic or mechanical, including photocopying, recording, or by any information storage and retrieval system, without permission in writing from the copyright holder.

TABLE OF CONTENTS

DEDICATION

We dedicate this vision and pastoral plan

to Catholic young adults—men and women in their

late teens, twenties, and thirties. We do so because

we realize the tremendous gifts that they bring

to church life. As single people or married couples,

with or without children, their presence enriches our

society and our Church. We hope this plan will be

an effective tool to connect young adults with

Jesus Christ and his challenge to bring the

Gospel—with its message of hope—to society.

PREFACE

A Message to Young Adults

Dear Brothers and Sisters,

s we began to write this pastoral plan we chose first to meet with some of you. These meetings, where you shared the joys and struggles of your daily life, have been a time of grace and understanding for us. We applaud your desire to belong to a community that shares similar convictions and to learn more about sacred Scripture, tradition and the teachings of the Church. We acknowledge the pain many of you speak of in feeling unwelcome and alone—strangers in the house of God. For any failure to extend hospitality, we apologize and promise greater efforts to welcome you into church life. We hope that anyone who enters a Catholic church for Mass, or at any other time, will feel comfortable and welcome. We also acknowledge that some of you recently have joined the Church. We welcome you. Others of you may be tempted to leave. We regret this. What you have told us presents the Church with both a challenge and an opportunity for our ministry.

We know that your talents, and those of other young adults, can enrich the Church and can be a sign of God's presence in society. We invite you to share them with us and to become part of a welcoming community for other young adults as well. Not too long ago our Holy Father spoke of your importance to the life of the Church: "The Church needs your energies, your enthusiasm, your ideals, in order to make the Gospel of life penetrate the fabric of society, transforming people's hearts and the structures of society in order to create a civilization of true justice and love."[1]

We also heard you speak of the difficulty in making moral decisions. We pledge to work with you to provide effective Catholic education and faith formation for you and other young adults. We want to share the Church's rich history and tradition with you. We want to provide opportunities for you to explore the Scriptures so the word of God becomes alive in your hearts. It is not easy to live as a Christian in contemporary society.

The influences of media and some elements of popular culture do not always support Christian values. People can have convictions that are opposed to what we cherish. We are challenged to let the Gospel, rather than society or popular culture, define what it means to live a successful life. We are also aware that many young adults are approached aggressively by various spiritual and religious movements that perceive our religion as inadequate or wrong. Probably some people with whom you work or go to college will challenge what you believe. Appreciate your faith. Stand firm in your beliefs. Help those who do not believe in Jesus Christ discover the beauty of a life based on the Gospel.

In a special way, we would like to speak to those men and women in difficult situations: to those who are unemployed or underemployed, who have been abused, who experience discrimination because of economic or ethnic prejudices, who struggle with their sexuality, who are newcomers to our country, who are struggling in their marriage, who seek wisdom and guidance in raising children, or who are having difficulty making and keeping commitments. We want you to know that you are not alone and that we will continue our efforts to listen to your concerns and speak on your behalf, offering you a hope rooted in the embrace of Jesus Christ.

During your life journey, continue to hope and to dream. We want to support you in every way we can, even as we acknowledge that this support has not always been present. This is one of the works of the Christian community—to help you live your life in Jesus Christ. Do not hesitate to make Jesus the center of your life, the focus of your choices in life. In the words of our Holy Father, "Build your lives on the one model that will not deceive you . . . open the Gospel and discover that Jesus Christ wants to be your 'friend' (cf. Jn 15:14). He wants to be your 'companion' at every stage on the road of life (cf. Lk 24:13-35). He wants to be the 'way,' your path through the anxieties, doubts, hopes and dreams of happiness (cf. Jn 14:6). He wants to be your God (cf. Mt 16:13-17)."[2]

You have so many gifts to offer the Church: your faith, your desire to serve, your spiritual hunger, your vitality, your optimism and idealism, your talents and skills. We can all learn from you, so we ask you to expand your leadership role in witnessing to the Gospel on campus. . . . We look forward to working more closely with you to make the Church ever more effective in announcing the reign of God.

A Letter to College Students from the Catholic Bishops of the United States, 1995, p. 5

We would like to share with you the words of one of your peers, a young woman who wrote to us from New York. She sums up what so many of you have told us and how we hope the Church can be present in your lives.

As a young adult in today's dynamic society, I—like so many other young adults—am hungry. I have felt a strong spiritual hunger, a hunger that stems from the need to discover who I am, who is my God, and what is my purpose in society. It is a hunger that once fed can continue to fuel my life journey in a direction that would follow the footsteps of Christ.

It is my hope that the Catholic Church will help guide me through this transitional period of my life; to keep me in touch with the "big picture" of life while I strive to pursue both my immediate and distant dreams; to help me find peace along the way. It is also my hope that the Catholic Church will provide us, as young adults, with the opportunities to truly feel an integral and necessary part of the church community; to provide us the chance to gather with other young adults so that we may share and reflect on our life journey and self-discovery together.

I believe that through a community of encouragement and support based on the life and teachings of Christ, the Catholic Church can give me the inspiration, strength, and perseverance necessary to continue my journey and to realize my hopes and dreams for life.

Michelle M. Mystkowski, Patchogue, N.Y.

In meeting you, the young adult members of the Church, we are more aware of your capability to love and serve. We invite you to continue to give of yourself, your time, your energies, and your talents for the good of others. We will be praying that the Holy Spirit guide you and the Church as together we grow in the love of Jesus Christ. We promise to walk with you and with all people who love life. In doing this, you will be sons and daughters of the light—a light of hope for the Church, for our country, and for all humanity!

The Catholic Bishops of the United States

INTRODUCTION TO THE PASTORAL PLAN

"Sons and Daughters of the Light"*

You are the light of the world. A city built on a hilltop cannot be hidden. No one lights a lamp to put it under a tub; they put it on the lampstand where it shines for all in the house. In the same way your light must shine, . . . so that, seeing your good works, they may give praise to your Father in heaven.

(Mt 5:14-16)

WHY WE ARE ISSUING THIS PLAN

In every age, Jesus Christ is the light of all nations (*Lumen Gentium*, no. 1) with Christian men and women called to reflect the light of Christ and, in this way, to be "light" for the world. To reflect the light of Christ requires a maturity of faith and a willingness to live this faith daily in society. We join the Holy Father in affirming the essential dignity of young adult men and women—those in their late teens, twenties, and thirties—as "sons and daughters of the light." Yet, many young adults tell us that they face increasingly complex and difficult times and that they need the help of the Catholic Christian community to be this "light."

They tell us about changes in family life, church life, societal values, and neighborhoods. They highlight how these, along with advances in technology, communications, and medicine, present new and different problems and require new and different responses. We bishops recognize these changes and realize that we must address them together in the Church if we are to share the faith with the next generation.

We begin by acknowledging that at the center of our faith is the belief that all people, made in the image and likeness of God in Christ, are called to be sons and daughters of God—lights for the world. Through this plan, we hope to accomplish three things:

1

> **Y**oung adults hunger and thirst for God. We desire to experience Christ's love in our own lives that we may live lives of hope. As we develop our spiritual life, we look for three things. First, we search out meaningful experiences of liturgy. . . . Second, we seek to learn more about our faith. Third, we are eager to share our personal stories in a small Christian community of friends. . . .
>
> *Sergio Rodgrigues, Providence, R.I.*

1. To state firmly that we, as members of the Church, must actively invite and welcome young adults into the life of the Church. This does not mean placing special emphasis on one generation but having a vision of Church rooted in God's invitation to all generations.

2. To describe briefly the life situation of young adults so the Church can respond effectively to their needs and concerns.

3. To develop a comprehensive and workable plan of action for ministering with people in their late teens, twenties, and thirties based on the four goals of connecting young adults with Jesus Christ, the Church, the mission of the Church in the world, and a community of their peers.

We recognize a certain urgency in developing this plan as a result of the listening sessions with young adults. These sessions provided us with valuable insights and knowledge concerning the Church's ministry with young adults. In particular, the following points deserve our attention:

• Many young adults are willing to share their leadership skills in ministry and their deep spirituality with their new parish communities. For some, these gifts developed during their college years through participation in campus ministry.

• There is a growing interest among young adults, on campus and in the workplace, to devote time and energy to helping others through community service activities.

• Many young adults express a desire to develop a closer relationship with Jesus Christ and to deepen their spiritual life, but this does not necessarily mean being a member of a Church.

• During late adolescence and early twenties, many men and women, while claiming to be Catholic, decide to participate less in church activities, especially the Sunday eucharist.[3]

• With the birth of their first child, young adults typically return to active religious practice after a decline in church participation during late adolescence and their early twenties. Today this return is no longer certain. If they do return, it can be with great tentativeness.

• There is a growing movement away from an institutional conception of religion to an individual conception of faith. This is particularly true for those born in the 1970s and 1980s.[4]

- Many Catholic young adults seeking a welcoming community and answers to questions about the meaning of life are attracted to religious/spiritual movements, sects and cults, and fundamentalist churches.

- Many Catholic men and women tell of not feeling welcomed in our communities, while others speak of wanting, but not finding, the Church's help with serious moral and economic questions.

- People from different ethnic groups sometimes struggle to express their faith in terms of their culture.[5]

- The membership of many, if not most, of our Catholic organizations is much older today than it was twenty years ago.

- Interchurch marriages have increased. This ultimately affects church life, especially as a couple decides how to worship and then raise their children in a religious tradition.[6]

- The values of many young adults no longer come primarily from family and Church but from friends, the media, and contemporary society.

- Many young adults feel they do not have the same access to economic and social opportunities as their parents. This affects their faith, hopes, and dreams for the future.

- Young adults who suffer from violence and poverty come from other countries to the United States looking for peace and for ways to make a living. They hope that their quality of life will improve in this new land.

In light of these insights, our ministry with young adults, who make up approximately 30 percent of the total U.S. population, must be intensified.[7] We need to be a Church that is interested in the lives of these men and women and is willing to invite them into our community. We need to be a Church imbued with a missionary zeal for the Gospel. When young adults accept our invitation, we must welcome them, acknowledge their participation, and make room for them in all aspects of church life. This outreach is especially important to the alienated. The words of Pope Paul VI speak of the importance of this ministry: "Existing circumstances suggest to us that we should devote our attention in particular to young people. . . . It is essential that young people themselves . . . should be ever more zealous in their apostolate to their contemporaries. The Church relies greatly on such help from young people, and we ourselves have repeatedly expressed our full confidence in them."[8]

THE AUDIENCE FOR THE PASTORAL PLAN

This plan is written to people in leadership positions in church life to encourage them to recognize, support, and motivate ministry with, by, and for young adults. This includes those in parishes, campus ministry centers, dioceses, the military, and Catholic movements and organizations. It is especially written

- to pastors and pastoral associates, to encourage them to give special attention to the needs of young adults in their parishes.

- to campus ministers, to strengthen the relationship between campus and parish.

- to young adult ministers, who work most directly with young adults, to recognize the efforts they have made and to incorporate their ministry into the full life of the Church.

- to young adults in leadership positions within the Church who work among their peers and with the larger community.

- to diocesan offices, especially those that work with ethnic and immigrant populations, many of whom are people in their late teens, twenties, and thirties.

- to military chaplains, who have a unique opportunity and challenge since a large group of Catholic young adults is found in the military.

- to leaders in parishes, movements, and organizations whose ministry connects them to young adults, such as chaplains (in schools, healthcare centers, and in prisons), family life ministers, parochial vicars, directors of religious education, youth ministers, those involved in liturgical ministries, adult educators (especially those who prepare people for marriage, baptism, the Rite of Christian Initiation of Adults, and lay ministry), and parish council members.

As a body is one though it has many parts, and all the parts of the body, though many, are one body, so also Christ. For in one spirit we were all baptized into one body . . . If [one] part suffers, all the parts suffer with it; if one part is honored, all the parts share its joy.

1 Cor 12:12-13, 26

PART

The Young Adult

ONE

WHO ARE YOUNG ADULTS?

As we mentioned in our dedication, young adulthood refers to people in their late teens, twenties, and thirties; single, married, divorced, or widowed; and with or without children.[9] They are present in every trade and profession. They live in the many communities that make up our society—from rural areas to small towns to large metropolitan areas. They come from diverse cultural, ethnic, educational, vocational, social, political, and spiritual realities. This diversity is reflected in the large number of people from various nations coming to this country whose median age is in the early to mid-twenties.[10]

Young adults were raised with music, television, and the rapid explosion of information and technology. They are a generation that some social scientists call the first truly multicultural and multimedia generation.[11] They live in a society where access to technology can easily determine one's potential for success. More than previous generations, they feel the widening separation between those who have access to resources and those who are denied such resources because of poverty, lack of education, and discrimination.

Young adults undertake numerous developmental tasks as they continue to grow and mature.[12] Many first experience autonomy and discover new roles in family, work, society, and the Church as they begin college, their first job, or marriage. Today many young adults spend longer periods in transition. Marriage is delayed; children come later in life; geographic and job mobility is high; and second and third careers are common. Some find themselves single again through separation, divorce, or the death of a spouse. Some may find themselves raising children alone. When we consider all these factors, it is easy to understand why many young adults believe that life today is different. An effective ministry pays attention to these issues.

TASKS OF YOUNG ADULTHOOD

During our meetings, young adults spoke of many concerns, which can be grouped into four key areas: *personal identity, relationships, work,* and *spiritual life.* While these concerns are not new to young adults, life today is different in two ways: these tasks are undertaken over an extended period of time, for some, into their thirties; and there is a lack of family, civic, and pastoral institutions to support them.

DEVELOPING PERSONAL IDENTITY

While individuals continue to mature throughout life, various new experiences influence the development of personal identity. These new experiences include employment, changing relationships with the family of origin, a continuous maturation or "ownership" of their faith, leaving the family home and possibly relocating to another area, affirmation of ethnic and cultural identity, and development of new relationships at work, at home, or on campus. Many young adults—some for the first time—meet people of different faiths, values, cultures, and sexual orientation. When they meet this broader mix of people, young

adults can, at times, find their values and beliefs challenged.

During this time, young adults also learn how to accomplish tasks and work independently, move toward interdependence and become comfortable asking others for help, and choose and act on personal values that give meaning to life.[13]

As a single woman in my late twenties, I have found myself working and living in a society in which family and community are, for a variety of reasons, devalued. Situations such as divorce, fear of strangers, economic hardship, violence, and the uncertainty of the job market, which often require movement and relocation, have combined to set the stage for a social atmosphere filled with separation and division.

Elizabeth Sheehan, Mumford, N.Y.

Today, exploring and developing one's ethnicity is particularly significant. While this self-identification is true for all people, it is especially important for recent immigrants and for those born in the United States who are now third and fourth generation. This involves becoming comfortable with one's culture of origin and understanding its history.[14] It is achieving a balance between one's particular ethnic group and the culture at large.

DEVELOPING RELATIONSHIPS

Most young adults experience changes in their relationships. Existing friendships may deepen, and they may make new friends among a broader mix of people. At the same time, they are reordering the relationships within their family, integrating sexuality into their lives, and choosing a permanent lifestyle such as marriage or a vocation to the priesthood, diaconate, or religious life.

Making Friends and Developing Intimacy

During the young adult years, friendships that developed during adolescence often change. Some relationships deepen, others fade. At the same time, new relationships are formed within ethnic communities and around church activities, hobbies, sports, work, or school. Many young adults with small children become friends with parents of other small children through school or community activities, thereby forming small communities for support and information. Some single young adults make friends through the workplace, church, or the health club while others speak of the pain of being alone in a crowd. These young adults, who are not able to surround themselves with friends and family, struggle with much loneliness.

Developing Multicultural Relationships

Young adults navigate another new challenge as they develop friendships among people of diverse cultures. Through these experiences, they seek to understand their own culture while becoming sensitive to the many cultures around them. Through these friendships, the barriers that separate culture from culture and create divisions among people can begin to break down. As a result, prejudice and discrimination lessen, and understanding and compassion increase. People can freely and consciously integrate elements of their culture of origin with the culture at large into a new vision that is founded on a coherent system of values and beliefs.[15]

Reordering of Relationships within the Family of Origin

The relationships that young adult men and women have with their parents change as they move into a more adult relationship with them. While these changes signal a reordering within the family, it will always be true that "the family and the home are where we learn who we are. It is the family that teaches us much about ourselves. It is the family that is the first school and the first laboratory for the transmission of culture, the passing on of values, the handing down of traditions, the planting of the seed of faith and the proclamation of the Good News."[16]

> As a mother of a son and a daughter entering adulthood, I know that love is much more than what I say to them . . . it is what I do, and it is what I model. . . . I know that a parent's love takes new shapes and a new presence during this time in their lives. . . .
>
> Carolyn Adrian, Victoria, Texas

Many young adults who during their adolescence sought independence and a certain distance from parents begin to appreciate them in a new way—as role models, mentors, and friends. Others must come to terms with patterns of destructive family behavior that resulted from substance and other abuses during their childhood and adolescent years. A few young adults even become the economic and emotional support for their parents.

> One of my dreams is that both parents and children would become better friends, sharing more and communicating better within an atmosphere of trust, participating in the life of the Church, and creating a more Christian community. We can all be witnesses of the living Christ.
>
> Eduardo Pincena, Texas

Many young adults struggle with the tension between differences in contemporary culture and the cultural heritage of their families. Young adults from diverse cultures have "distinct and unique perspectives, values and traditions relating to family and family life"[17] that they wish to preserve. Because of the process of acculturation, this can result in struggles between generations over which traditions to keep and which to adapt or combine.[18]

Integrating Sexuality into Life

As they engage in and deepen their relationships with others, young adults seek to integrate sexuality into their lives. They seek to discern how their values and religious beliefs should inform their decisions around sexuality. Because of such pervasive practices as nonmarital intercourse, living together outside of marriage, and sexual abuse, many express concern about how to sustain a positive attitude and Christian wisdom regarding sexuality.

Choosing to Marry

During the young adult years, many men and women marry and begin a family. Many newly married couples speak of delaying the start of a family to deepen their relationship, to find work, or to become more financially stable. Some tell us that they value children but wonder about bringing children into a world marked with so much pain and evil. Couples from different cultures face challenges identifying which traditions and customs to follow and deciding how to raise their children.

Others are concerned with marital stability in a society where nearly one-half of the marriages end in separation or divorce. They know from the experiences of divorced parents, grandparents, siblings, and friends that this experience is very painful. They approach marriage seriously. Some speak of the challenge of raising children as a single parent. Others share the pain of being separated from full communion with the church community as a result of remarriage or being in relationships not recognized by the Church.

The Single Life

Another difference in the lives of young adults today is the number of men and women who remain single throughout their lifetime. For some, this is a conscious decision to focus their lives on their careers or work or to dedicate themselves to others through community service. Others remain single because they do not find compatible spouses. The experience can be very painful, but it can also lead the single person to a greater level of maturity.

Single young adults have very different needs and interests from those who are engaged or married, with or without children. These single men and women work to identify what gives meaning to their lives in a way that is different from those who are married or have a religious vocation. The quest for close friendships and participation in small groups or communities of like people is particularly important. Young adults form these relationships even while realizing that they may be temporary, due to the transient nature of young adult life.

DEVELOPING A MEANING OF WORK

Young adulthood often signals a person's entrance into the world of work. "What do you do for a living?" is a constant topic of conversation because work is a major part of their lives. For young adults, this experience is highly fluid because they move from job to job and even from career to career. Work can dictate their use of time and can determine what they can afford to do or buy. It can also determine the quality and quantity of leisure time. Work defines and influences a young adult's identity and self-concept and is a prime place where friendships and other relationships develop because generally it is not done alone.

Young men and women speak of work as fulfilling a function and providing meaning. Work allows young adults to meet their practical needs but even more importantly to seek meaning and

fulfillment of their dreams and visions. Although work may not help achieve their dreams, it is important for young adults to nurture a vision, learn how to work in a truly personal and life-giving way, and to continue to discern God's call.[19]

> The Christian, whether laborer or judge, doctor or farmer, business person or professor, is recognized by the way he or she practices the commandment of love for God and neighbor.... Whatever place you take in society, whatever profession you carry out, you are called to do as a service.
>
> *Papal Message to College Students at Villa Nazareth in Rome, June 8, 1996*

Work as Functional

For many, work has a purely functional role; it is what puts food on the table, provides shelter, and takes care of the family. Today both husbands and wives often work. Some couples do so to survive economically; others to establish careers. This can greatly influence a couple's relationship with each other, family, friends, and the Church. Many young adults are concerned about unemployment, underemployment, and job-related stress during these years. Work can take on another dimension when young adults realize that they may remain single or be a single parent for life. This can lead to concerns about financial security and a focus on work over relationships.

Work as Meaningful

In Christian theology, work is directed to bringing the Gospel to the world. It can give meaning to our lives and can provide an opportunity to collaborate with God in building a culture of life within society. Meaning in work comes through choosing a career, volunteering, and discerning a vocation.

Finding a fulfilling career and a good job is a principal reason why many young adults go to college, attend a trade school, or immigrate to this country. More than in the past, young men and women must work hard at finding a job that is meaningful, fits their career goal, and is financially rewarding. Many young adults end up accepting work that is less fulfilling but is able to sustain them economically. Others choose work that pays less in order to find employment in a chosen field. Many people who work for the Church or in service/social justice agencies are living examples of this willingness to forgo economic benefits in order to fulfill a dream.

Work includes not only what one does to earn a living and support a family but also countless hours and energy spent volunteering one's time and talent within the social, civic, and church community. Today, more people of all ages seek volunteer work as a way of meeting people and contributing to the community.

Young adults participate in volunteer work for a number of reasons, sometimes because of the difficulty of getting a job but more often out of the desire to be of service. Volunteering is an avenue where people can achieve their dream of contributing to the common good—of making a difference in the world today and embracing an enlarged vision of the world and their role as citizens. This leads some to join service organizations and to serve as locally elected officials or as members of civic review boards and homeowner associations. Sometimes this participation is to effect social change, including the transformation of unjust situations. Volunteering touches the experiential side of life where it can be most helpful to men and women who are in the process of discerning God's calling.

The ultimate search for a meaning and a spirituality of work in a Christian context is a response to God's call, which is our vocation. This response reflects the spiritual dimension of work. God calls each of us to spread the Gospel through a particular vocation. An important decision for young adults is the discernment of this call. In the past, young people made a vocation choice typically during late adolescence or their early twenties. Today many men and women undertake this discernment in their twenties and thirties, often leading to a decision to marry, remain single, or embrace a vocation to the priesthood, diaconate, religious life, or lay ministry.

DEVELOPING
A SPIRITUAL LIFE

What does it mean for young adults to be a "spiritual" person? Our listening sessions with young adults paint a picture of four characteristics.

1. Grappling with questions about the purpose of life and what it means to be a good person.

2. Appropriating and internalizing the gift of faith and a religious tradition.

3. Finding an adult faith community in which to live.

4. Developing an "inner life" to correspond to an "outer life."

> *As a young boy growing up in the Catholic Church, I was taught to seek out the truth about life, to find those things that exemplified the highest ideals in life, and let my life, in turn, be characterized by those high ideals.*
>
> Robert J. Dougherty, Okla.

These characteristics can be expressed as a desire of young adults to root their lives in something that gives them hope and conveys meaning. Their search for a personal identity, pursued in relationships and work, partially satisfies this hunger for meaning. However, time and time again they told us of their thirst for a relationship with God. They ask, "What is the purpose of my life? What do I live for?"

Young adult men and women experience a spiritual tension arising from the contrast between contemporary society and the desire to live according to the will of God. They speak at times of a wariness toward organized religion. Although they desire a deeper spiritual life, this attitude and other influences from contemporary society push them to question and doubt what has been part of their lives. The Church needs to respond to this doubting and questioning by encouraging a dialogue that welcomes challenges from the young adult to the Church and from the Church to the young adult, so that each may grow in discipleship.

Young adults gradually come to understand this searching as a dynamic between faith and life. Each person internalizes this according to his or her own family history and cultural roots. Asians, Hispanics, and Latinos see their spirituality springing from their relationship with God, community, faith, and culture. African American men and women see spirituality as "rooted in the African tradition and in the historical and cultural experience of black Americans."[20] A common thread is the understanding of spirituality as a "way of life of a people, a movement by the Spirit of God, and the grounding of one's identity as a Christian in every circumstance of life."[21]

Some experience this searching as a quiet inner questioning, a thoughtful reexamination of traditional beliefs. Others accomplish this by learning more about their faith or by participating in prayer groups and small communities. For still others, this searching can lead to a functional atheism, a rejection of organized religion, or a distancing from church activities and worship. This questioning should be seen as a path that leads to possible future faith development.

During this period of searching, there are many challenges. College students, along with those in the work force, speak of having their faith challenged by fundamentalists or agnostics. Many are attracted to these people because of the conviction present in their message. Others speak of being challenged by secular messages portrayed through television, music, movies, and the news media. Some even speak of the pain they experience from parishes that are inhospitable or unresponsive to their concerns and struggles.

> Spirituality develops and is nourished through culture which "primarily expresses how people live and perceive the world, one another, and God. Culture is the set of values by which a people judge, accept, and live what is considered important within the community.
>
> National Pastoral Plan for Hispanic Ministry, U.S. Catholic Bishops, no. 10

Despite the turbulence of these years, many seek to return to their faith, remembering the positive experiences of youth and campus ministry. They tell us that it is our tradition that feeds their hunger. They return seeking participation and involvement in church life and guidance for their lives. Young adults need opportunities to share their stories and be affirmed in the importance of their lives within the Church. What is important to them and holds great value is being with people who have similar beliefs.[22] This common bond, shared within a community of peers and others, provides support and nourishment for their faith. The Church needs to provide young adults with the support, prayer, time, and space to search fruitfully and to nurture the movement toward deeper faith.[23]

No matter the form, it is important to realize that this questioning is a searching for what it means to be sons and daughters of the light. What a wonderful opportunity this presents to the Church.

Everyone in the Church, precisely because they are members, receives and thereby shares in the common vocation to holiness.

Christifideles Laici, no.16

PART
A Vision of Faith for
Young Adults
TWO

What can the Church offer to fulfill the spiritual hunger of young adults? The Church can offer them a vision of life based on a faith that calls each of them to holiness, community, and service. In the previous section, we discussed what life is like for young adults today. Now we wish to share a vision of how this life can be lived through the lens of Christian faith, where young adults see their search for identity, relationships, work, and spiritual life in relation to Christ's call to holiness, community, and service. We want to paint a picture of what it means for young adults to make a commitment to Jesus Christ. This commitment begins by accepting God's call to life with him. It is nourished through a community of faith where we grow in holiness. It is lived daily as each person works to transform the world according to God's plan.

ACCEPTING GOD'S INVITATION

Our faith tells us that goodness is possible because God acts for us. God chooses us and plants the desire for himself in every human heart. God invites us to be transformed into holy people, to

> *The Church, as community, carries out the work of Jesus by entering into the cultural, religious, and social reality of the people . . . she is able to preach the need for conversion of everyone, to affirm the dignity of the human person, and to seek ways to eradicate personal sin, oppressive structures, and forms of injustice.*
>
> National Pastoral Plan for Hispanic Ministry, no. 13

participate and find support in a community of believers, and to make this transformation happen by continually saying "yes" to Jesus' invitation to "Come, follow me" (Lk 18:22). This "yes" means, in the words of Aida Salgado, a young adult from Texas, "to share with others the Christ that came down from the cross to make his dwelling inside each of us." It is becoming people of great faith—sons and daughters of the light.

It is this deepening of one's spirituality through faith in Jesus Christ that provides the foundation and lens for life. In a world of shifting values, Jesus Christ offers us a solid foundation. He is the one constant who will not change. In times of confusion and doubt, our commitment to follow the lead of Jesus Christ can bring us a hope-filled

vision for our world. In the midst of life's many and unpredictable changes, the Church's tradition resounds with God's hopes and dreams for young adults.

THE CALL TO HOLINESS—GROWING IN JESUS CHRIST

What does it mean to be *a holy* or *spiritual* person? Simply put, it is God's call to be in union with Christ. "You have been told . . . what is good, and what the Lord requires of you: Only to do the right and to love goodness, and to walk humbly with your God" (Mi 6:8). To be holy is to live according to the Gospel—to be grounded in Christ Jesus. It is the ever-present challenge to be a people of heartfelt compassion, kindness, humility, gentleness, patience, and forgiveness (cf. Col 3:12). It is a call to embrace the beatitudes—to be poor in spirit, to comfort, to be meek, to be merciful, to be peacemakers (see Mt 5:3-11). It entails listening and meditating on the word of God and actively participating in the eucharist and the sacramental life of the Church. It is to pray individually and as a community and to pray often.[24] It is an invitation to bring a heightened sense of the presence of Jesus Christ into the regular rhythms of life: going to school or work, raising a family, and participating in civic life.

The journey toward holiness is the path toward finding and satisfying our hunger for meaning, making something worthwhile out of our lives. It urges us to reach beyond ourselves in service to our families and other relationships, to our work, to our communities, and to our Church; to be zealous in the pursuit of justice for the poor, the marginalized, the unborn, the elderly, the suffering, and the brokenhearted. "The vocation to love, understood as true openness to our fellow human beings and solidarity with them, is the most basic of all vocations. It is the origin of all vocations in life."[25] It is inseparable from our love for God.[26]

This deepening of faith in Jesus Christ leads us to a vision of what life can be. It may require acts of courage to accomplish great things for humanity. During this journey, we do not travel alone. We share with all believers the struggle: "I'm on the battlefield for my Lord. I promise him that I will serve him till I die" (African Spiritual). The "call to holiness is [then] a gift from the Holy Spirit. [Our] response is a gift to the Church and to the world."[27]

THE CALL TO COMMUNITY— NOURISHING FAITH

The challenge of being transformed into a holy person is not undertaken alone but within a faith community. Young adults repeatedly told us of their desire to find and to participate in communities that accept and welcome them, where people hold values and beliefs similar to their own. This longing for community touches each of us at the very core of our being. It is basic to being human, not "an extraneous addition, but a requirement" of our nature.[28] Within the community, we develop our potential, foster our talents, form our identity, and respond to the many challenges of being holy men and women. Community is not only an abstract principle

Today's young adults are at a disadvantage. . . . There is a story and a face with each one of these lives. . . . We are the generation that has grown up in broken families. We have gay and lesbian friends who want to be accepted for who they are. We have friends struggling with their sexuality yet feel as if they cannot discuss it. We have friends and family members who are divorced; we have friends who are single and pregnant. . . .

Matthew T. Dunn, Beavercreek, Ohio

but also a concrete reality lived each day at home, on campus, within society, and in organizations, movements, and parishes.

Community is God's promise to those who have accepted the gracious invitation to live the Gospel and to be lights for the world. Claimed by Christ and baptized into the Holy Spirit, all have become full members of the Church, worthy of the love, the respect, and the support of the entire Christian community.[29] This communion of faith is a *communion of charisms*, of gifts and talents, a place where young adults participate not only as receivers but also as contributors.[30] This communion of the Church, rooted in God's love, offers young adults the vision, purpose, and foundation for the healing that they long for in the midst of life's painful experiences.

People of all ages voice the need for reconciliation and healing as a result of failed relationships, abuse and addictions, sexual permissiveness, violence on the streets, broken or violent homes, unemployment, discrimination in all of its forms, rejection, and loneliness. Christ's redemption is the basis for this healing. The community of faith is the place where the healing power of Jesus touches people and, through them, our neighborhoods, cities, and society. In the sacraments—especially reconciliation and the eucharist—young adults meet the healing presence of the Lord and receive the strength and the grace to confront the many challenges of living a Christian lifestyle.

The call to Christian holiness and community demands a mutuality of relationships. As young adults strive to grow ever more faithful to their new life in Christ, so too the whole Church endeavors to celebrate the gift of her young adults. The Church recognizes the Holy Spirit working through them in their energy, creativity, participation, and leadership.

In the same way, we are called to hear their pain. The Church must be open to learn from their experiences, anxieties, uncertainties, and honest and constructive questioning. "The joy and hope, the grief and anguish . . . especially of those who are poor or afflicted in any way, are the joy and

> *I feel that the Church can be a place where young adults return for reassurance during our critical times of insecurity and searching. We need a safe place to talk about faith, or lack of faith, and a community to support us and let us know that examination and uncertainty are all part of the journey.*
>
> Heather Thomae, Little Rock, Ark.

hope, the grief and anguish of the followers of Christ as well."[31]

THE CALL TO SERVICE— LIVING FAITH IN THE WORLD

The challenge of faith is to be a credible witness to the power of the Gospel in the world today. We are inspired by the stories of young adults whose enthusiasm and service build up the reign of God on earth. Their thirst for knowledge, their efforts to maintain a life of integrity, their respect for differences among all peoples, their care for their children and the unborn, and their service through volunteer and missionary activity all form a worthy testament to the role of young adults in living out their faith.

We have spoken on several occasions about the call to Christian adulthood, most recently in our document on the laity entitled *Called and Gifted for the Third Millennium*. There we highlighted the many marks of a mature Christian: an awareness of the significance of education, especially the ability to make good decisions based on the teachings of the Church; the necessity for adult catechesis and other means of faith development; the importance of discerning one's talents in order to exercise them more effectively; learning to live with mystery and ambiguity; and participation in family, neighborhood, government, and society in ways that bring the gospel principles of justice, compassion, and mercy truly alive. These aspects of Christian maturity call all men and women to an understanding that "we are called to be faithful, not necessarily successful."[32]

For young adults, as for all Catholic adults, the Catholic faith is lived in the "ordinary dynamics of life—caring for a family, job responsibilities, exercising duties of citizenship."[33] This is what discipleship is all about. The world is the place where men and women fulfill their Christian vocation. The mission of the Church is not directed at itself, but at nurturing and forming people who "are called by God so that they, led by the spirit of the Gospel, might contribute to the sanctification of the world, as from within like leaven, by fulfilling their own particular duties."[34]

Through the call to holiness, community, and service through lived faith, the whole Church provides the necessary support for young adults to be disciples of Christ living their faith, nourished by the Church, and proclaiming with the prophets of old: "The spirit of the Lord is upon me, because he has anointed me to bring glad tidings to the poor. He has sent me to proclaim liberty to captives and recovery of sight to the blind, to let the oppressed go free, and to proclaim a year acceptable to the Lord (Lk 4:18-19).

As I responded to the call of Christ found through prayer, Scripture, and church tradition, I decided that the only true response for these gifts would be one of service. . . . I began to teach other young adults about that which helped me so much. . . . I watched many young adults begin to seriously grapple with their own faith questions and then begin to seriously follow Christ.

Lisa Klewicki, Glendale, Calif.

The person who has been evangelized goes on to evangelize others. Here lies the test of truth, the touchstone of evangelization; it is unthinkable that a person should accept the Word and give himself to the Kingdom without becoming a person who bears witness to it and proclaims it in his turn.

Evangelii Nuntiandi, no. 24

PART

A Plan for Ministry

THREE

INTRODUCTION: THE CHURCH'S MINISTRY WITH YOUNG ADULTS

The Catholic Church has always sought to provide ministry to people in their late teens, twenties, and thirties through marriage preparation, campus ministry, Catholic singles groups, military chaplaincies, and participation in various organizations and movements. Young adult ministry itself, as a designated area of pastoral care, has been part of church life in many dioceses for over fifteen years. This plan applauds these efforts and seeks to develop a more intentional ministry based on this foundation.

In the introduction, we stated that one of our goals is to strengthen the relationship of young adults with the Church. As in any relationship, we need to know each other, therefore we identified the tasks and issues concerning young adults. We also discussed how our faith provides a lens through which we can view life. Now we offer a plan based on the understanding of young adults in Part One and rooted in the vision of faith developed in Part Two. We also build this plan on the foundation of past strategies such as *Empowered by the Spirit*, the *National Pastoral Plan for Hispanic Ministry*, *Here I Am, Send Me*, and *Go and Make Disciples*, to name a few. We hope this plan assists you in your ministry to and with young adults.

The strategies contained in this section are not meant to be comprehensive, but to provide planners with a starting point. We believe that a successful outreach to young adults will achieve four goals. It will connect young adults with the following:

1. Jesus Christ;

2. the Church, by inviting and welcoming their presence in the Christian community;

3. the mission of the Church in the world;

4. a peer community in which their faith is nurtured and strengthened.

PRINCIPLES FOR MINISTRY WITH YOUNG ADULTS IN THE PARISH, THE DIOCESE, AND ON CAMPUS

The following principles are offered to guide the development of effective ministry with young adults. Keep these in mind when planning new pastoral initiatives or evaluating current ministries.

1. Young adults internalize their beliefs and values within a supportive community and live their vocation in the world.

2. Young adults seek opportunities for relationships with their peers and experiences that are intergenerational and multicultural.

3. Young adults understand both the message of faith and the traditions of the Church when these are communicated through words, symbols, and activities that relate to life experiences.

4. Young adults respond positively when the Church invites their participation and engages them in the planning of activities for the spiritual life of the community.

5. The Church meets young adults where they are present: the workplace, the home, the campus, and the civic community.

6. Effective ministry invites young adults into the life of the Church and collaborates with them to identify specific initiatives for the young adult community.

7. Effective ministry assists young adults to become spiritual people, thereby developing a holistic and healthy understanding of life and deepening one's relationship with God.

8. Effective ministry provides young adults with constructive opportunities to ask questions and to discover answers present in the teaching and tradition of the Catholic Church.

9. Effective ministry with young adults engages them in peer ministry, as well as family ministry.

10. Effective ministry acknowledges, understands, respects, and celebrates the cultural diversity of individuals and communities.

11. Effective ministry facilitates and engages young adults in an awareness of and an invitation to the work of justice, peace, and compassion.

12. Effective ministry includes the commitment of necessary resources for the evangelization, catechesis, and pastoral care of young adults.

The framework suggested in this section can be adapted to a variety of settings. Effective pastoral planning acknowledges the danger of designing a single approach in the expectation that it can respond adequately to all needs. This plan suggests a more dynamic and inclusive approach by involving young adults in the life of the local faith community and by developing specific initiatives within the young adult community.

> One of our dreams is to be supported and encouraged by the Church to carry out the commitment to our chosen vocation. We also hope the Church can be supportive of the many facets of our diversity. We hope the Church can incorporate the contributions of black Catholics into the Church's history . . . and abolish the notion of Blacks as new to Catholicism. We are eager to meet the challenges through assuming leadership roles, religious education, and actions of justice and peace.
>
> Henri M. Barnwell, Virginia Beach, Va.

THE PARISH AND YOUNG ADULTS

Often, the first community that Catholics connect with is the parish. This may be where they were baptized, where they stop by when they are in town, or where they hope to marry. Pastoral care for young adults requires that parishes be a *home* for young adults where they are personally touched in their faith journey. Here is where most young adults experience life cycle events—birth, marriage, and death—and struggle with the challenges of their lives—leaving home and coming back. The pastoral care of young adults demands a certain kind of openness and flexibility. Parish leaders need an awareness of the life patterns, transience, and mobility of young adults. Those who work with young adults will need an approach that is nonjudgmental yet challenging.

While this document acknowledges that ministry with young adults takes place in many different communities, a preeminent place is given to the parish. The goals, objectives, and strategies suggested in this document are specifically directed to the pastoral care of young adults in the parish community, but they can also be easily used or adapted for ministry on campuses or military bases, or within Catholic associations.

GOALS, OBJECTIVES, AND STRATEGIES

Ministry to and with Young Adults

We have identified four goals for ministry with young adults. These goals and the following objectives, along with the principles for ministry, should guide the diocese, parish, campus, military, and organization in developing practical plans for ministry to and with young adults.

GOAL ONE: CONNECTING YOUNG ADULTS WITH JESUS CHRIST

To foster the personal and communal growth and education of young adults toward a relationship with Jesus Christ leading to Christian maturity.

Objectives

Spiritual Formation and Direction: To help young adults develop their spiritual life rooted in a personal relationship with Jesus Christ as their redeemer and savior.

Religious Education/Formation: To help young adults appreciate the teachings and traditions of the Church through catechesis, religious education, and pastoral care.

Vocation Discernment: To help young adults understand vocation as primarily a call to holiness and Christian maturity lived through single or married life, the priesthood, the diaconate, or religious life.

Strategies to Implement Goal One

SPIRITUAL FORMATION AND DIRECTION

As mentioned earlier in this plan, young adults want to develop their spiritual life. They speak of this as being the foundation—the rootedness—of their lives. It is through this spiritual life that young adults grow in appreciation for the way God works in their lives. Some suggestions for helping young adults develop their spiritual life include the following:

In the next ten years, I will be making some of the biggest transitions of my life. I am not looking for a singles group to meet that special someone. I am searching for community. I am searching for people to share my journey. . . . I believe that the Church needs to actively reach out to young adults and give us the opportunity to find God at work in our lives. Our lives have become incredibly busy as we try to start careers, find jobs, and find ourselves. . . . My hope is that the Church would reach out to us—seek us out and open the door to participation. I am very aware of my need for God's forgiving love in my life. Yet it is so easy to put those needs on hold and focus on expectations that society has put on me. Having a community to share these struggles with would be a tremendous blessing.

Christopher J. Hood, New York, N.Y.

- Provide opportunities for participation in the sacraments, especially the sacraments of reconciliation, eucharist, confirmation, and anointing of the sick. Identify times that are convenient for young adult attendance.

- Provide opportunities for young adults to learn and experience different forms of personal and group prayer.

- Invite young adults from other faiths to gather together for ecumenical prayer.

- Form bible study and reflection groups that are both peer and intergenerational.

- Provide spiritual direction resources such as prayer and meditation books and audiotapes.

- Make available opportunities for personal spiritual direction/formation, and provide the necessary training of spiritual directors/facilitators.

- List in the parish or campus bulletin the name(s) of spiritual directors and/or confessors who are comfortable with young adults.

- Sponsor a variety of retreat opportunities for young adults to deepen their spirituality. These can be both group and/or individual experiences.

RELIGIOUS EDUCATION AND FORMATION

During the listening process, many young adults spoke of their desire for effective adult religious education to help them make good moral decisions. They said that they need a forum not only where misgivings and doubts can be expressed freely but also where the teachings of the Church can be clearly articulated in response. While some alienation stems from disagreement over church teachings, much of what young adults feel regarding the institutional Church arises from a misunderstanding of what the Church actually teaches. Many young adults told us that what is most convincing is an open but well-reasoned discussion, informed and fortified by the minister's confidence in the wisdom of the Church. Some suggestions for developing adult catechesis include the following:

- Offer a variety of both topical and programmatic formats such as a series of evening classes, special one-evening presentations, days of recollection/retreat, discussion groups, mentoring relationships, and missions.

- Develop catechetical options that best respond to the needs of the community such as Scripture study groups or RENEW-type formats.

- Use adult-centered methods that are compatible with the culture of the participants.

- Make available print resources, audio and videocassettes, and computer resources such as CD-ROM and the Internet. Audiotapes can be used while traveling, exercising, or at home in the evening.

- Choose themes for catechesis and faith formation that include church teaching or church life, such as church tradition, theology, theology of the sacraments, Scripture studies, the role of women in the Church, and Catholic identity. Also, consider issues that include relationships, intimacy, sexuality, family life, culture, workplace ethics, morality, personal faith, and dealing with life's pain.

The RCIA

The Rite of Christian Initiation of Adults (RCIA) is an excellent occasion to minister with young adults. The RCIA provides the opportunity for young adults to enter our faith and for those already baptized and in communion with the Church to be sponsors for other young adults. Parishes should continue to nourish the faith of these newly baptized. They also need to prepare young adults who have not received their first communion or been confirmed.

Marriage Preparation

For many young adults, marriage can be a key moment for evangelization. The engagement period itself is "set within the context of a rich evangelization process."[35] The Church connects with more young adults here than at any other time outside of Sunday Mass. They bring with them their past experiences of the Church. Some come with positive memories of parish youth ministry programs or Catholic schools. Others have been involved with the university or college campus ministry, but have limited connections to the parish. For some, this may be their first step back into church life.

Young adults approach the Church to be married for a number of reasons, including parental pressure, the desire to have a church wedding, or to reunite themselves with the Church. Regardless of why they come, the Church and its ministers need to welcome them as Christ welcomes them, with understanding, love, and acceptance, challenging them with the gospel message, and giving them hope that a lifelong commitment is possible.

Marriage preparation connects young adults with Christ and with the Church. The good news is that marriage preparation serves an important and useful purpose for most of those who participate in it.[36] Marriage preparation is an opportunity to learn more about the Church and its teachings, especially those pertaining to married life. It can be a "journey of faith which is similar to the catechumante (RCIA)."[37] Here are some key principles upon which to build strategies:

- Rejoice with couples as they make this commitment to each other for life; this is a very special moment in their lives.

- Challenge them lovingly and gently to greater growth in Jesus Christ rather than prejudge them.

- Present couples with a clear and dynamic presentation of authentic Catholic teaching on human sexuality, marriage, and family.

- Emphasize the sacramental dimension of marriage. While most engaged couples experience joy and life, as well as a certain amount of struggle, they may not connect those feelings to the gospel message.

- Help couples understand that the wedding is the beginning of a married life requiring continuous growth and understanding.

- Be sensitive to the cultural traditions of our diverse Catholic community—including those of the families of origin—when addressing questions of age, ritual/ceremony, and readiness.

- Be aware of the family dynamics of marriage preparation. Many unresolved issues between children and parents can come to the surface at this time. Weddings bring celebration and joy, but also stress and tension. Take every opportunity to encourage communication and, if necessary, reconcilation.

- Encourage couples to consider becoming involved in the parish where they are married or in the parish where they will be attending Mass.Invite active young couples to accompany them to their first parish event or service opportunity.

- Refrain from developing unnecessary rules and regulations that can alienate people of good will.

Here are some strategies for preparing couples for marriage:

- Involve clergy and married couples in the marriage preparation team—this approach is most effective. Invite the priest to play an active and substantial role.[38]

- Recruit married couples as mentors to meet with engaged couples. These mentors should be skilled in pastoral ministry with young adults and should understand the developmental tasks of people in their late teens, twenties, and thirties.

- Offer multi-session programs that include structured time for talking with each other. They can continue the dialogue between sessions.[39]

- Discuss subjects that are meaningful to engaged couples during marriage preparation such as theology of the sacrament, communication, commitment, conflict resolution, the role of religion (especially for interfaith marriages), values, children, and natural family planning.

- Use proven premarital inventory tools such as FOCUS or PREPARE.[40]

- Pray for couples in marriage preparation during the general intercessions at Mass and consider inviting engaged couples to receive a blessing from the community.

- Work collaboratively with the appropriate diocesan offices to administer different aspects of the marriage preparation program.

- Provide guidelines for marriage preparation and procedures for obtaining dispensations that are sensitive to the cultural implications of impediments and annulments, so confusion and misunderstanding are avoided. Pastoral ministers need to be aware of the pastoral application of these guidelines, which can be made available at campus centers, parishes, and military chaplancies.

The following are most helpful in clarifying church teaching on marriage and family: *The Documents of Vatican II, Familiaris Consortio, Letter to Families*, and recent documents from the Pontifical Council for the Family on human sexuality and marriage preparation.

Baptismal Preparation

As with marriage preparation, preparation for the sacrament of baptism of children is an opportunity to evangelize young adults and to strengthen their relationship with Christ and the Church. An effective preparation program continues the ongoing formation of parents and provides an opportunity for a closer relationship with their local community. Effective strategies include the following:

- Create opportunities for mutual support among parents seeking baptism for their children.

- Plan programs that take into consideration the time constraints of parents with infants and young children and that are sensitive to people's cultural traditions and practices of piety. Sunday morning may be more effective than an evening session.

- Be aware of and sensitive to those who have been married outside the Church. Baptismal preparation can begin a process of welcoming people back to the Church.

- Provide families with the opportunity to have their children baptized at a Sunday eucharistic celebration. For pastoral considerations, a separate celebration of the sacrament may be appropriate.

- Involve parents and family members in the ritual as much as possible. Consider providing a printed program to increase participation during the celebration of the sacrament.

> Do not be afraid to go out on the street and into public places like the first apostles, who preached Christ and the good news of salvation in the squares of cities, towns and villages. This is no time to be ashamed of the Gospel (cf. Rom 1:16). It is the time to preach it from the rooftops (cf. Mt 10:27).
>
> John Paul II, Homily at the WYD Vigil, 1993

VOCATION DISCERNMENT

As we discussed earlier, many men and women respond to God's call of vocation during young adulthood. Families, parishes, military chaplains, and campus ministers can help young people discern their vocations. In particular, consider these strategies:

- Hold seminars, workshops, and overnight retreats in a spritual setting to discuss vocation discernment, and commit resources for follow-up.

- Involve priests, deacons, religious, and lay ministers as mentors and spiritual guides for young men and women discerning their vocations.

- Develop a vocations committee in the parish, on the campus, or on the military base. Catholic organizations and movements can also develop vocations committees.

- Urge clergy to discuss vocations in their homilies and on other occasions.

- Invite young people to take a sabbatical year to do volunteer community service.

- Invite young adult coordinators to be members of the vocations team.

GOAL TWO: CONNECTING YOUNG ADULTS WITH THE CHURCH

To make contact with young adults and to invite and welcome them to participate in the life and mission of the Christian community, which proclaims Jesus Christ by preaching the Gospel.

Objectives

Evangelizing Outreach: To identify places where young adults gather and to connect them personally with the Church by listening to their concerns, hopes, and dreams and by welcoming them into a community of faith.

Forming the Faith Community: To invite, empower, and enable young adults to participate in the life of the Church through worship, community life, small faith communities, and evangelizing efforts, and on committees, in ministries, and in Catholic movements and organizations.

Pastoral Care: To provide activities, visitations, and counseling opportunities that respond to the spiritual and developmental needs of young adults.

> *Test everything, retain what is good.*
>
> 1 Thes 5:21.

Strategies to Implement Goal Two

EVANGELIZING OUTREACH

There are many opportunities to touch the lives of young adults, and these should be seen as moments for evangelizing outreach. Some of these may require a change in the way we approach evangelization so our outreach is more dynamic, taking the Church into the community where young adults gather rather than waiting for these men and women to come to us. Others include identifying situations where young adults already connect with the Church such as sacramental preparation programs and Sunday eucharist. Several strategies to consider include the following:

• Invite young adults into church life through personal contact, telephone calls, bulletin notices, letters, the Internet, and e-mail.

• Provide written materials in several languages and be sensitive to diverse ethnic traditions in order to reach young adults from different cultures.

• Encourage young adults who are involved in church life to invite their friends and other peers to community events.

• Identify places where young adults gather such as the workplace, shopping areas, health clubs, campuses, athletic fields, and civic associations,

and make time to be present at these places of gathering.

FORMING THE FAITH COMMUNITY

An Invitation to Participation

Throughout the history of the Church, people in their late teens, twenties, and thirties have been an active segment of church life. As our listening sessions indicated, that is not necessarily true today. Therefore, it is important to make an effort to invite and welcome them personally into church life. Young adults will participate when they perceive that the invitation is authentic and that their participation is constructive. Once the invitation is extended, it is important to match skills and talents with the needs of the community and to have a plan for follow-up. When ministering among young adults, remember the following:

• Young adults who are single will have different needs and concerns, and they have different life schedules than those who are married or married with children.

• Those who minister with young adults, including the parish staff and members of the parish council, may need specific training and orientation.

• The invitation to participate may need to be repeated. Young adults may not believe that they are truly being invited because of past experiences.

Some strategies for inviting young adults to participate in the faith community include the following:

• Develop, with young adults, activities and materials that specifically target their developmental needs, especially prayer groups and small Christian communities that place value on dialogue and shared communal experiences.

- Use community meetings and surveys to identify the concerns of young adults. Ask participating young adults to talk with and invite their friends and co-workers.

- Welcome and involve young adults in the planning of church events.

- Provide opportunities for recent college graduates or vacationing students to reconnect with the parish. Ask students who are home for the summer to assist as liturgical ministers, work with the youth program, be a summer catechist, or visit the sick or elderly. Host a gathering for new graduates and parishioners to learn more about becoming active within the life of the community.

Life-Giving Prayer and Worship

Liturgy is a key concern of young adults and is a primary meeting point with the Church. The quality of church life is often reflected in the prayerfulness and quality of its liturgy, which can be a connecting point between faith and life. One challenge to that connection is the need for the community to respect the diverse language traditions, spirituality, and piety of its many ethnic groups. Consistently, young adults speak of the life-giving power of good and prayerful liturgy and the pain and emptiness associated with poor liturgical experiences. They tell us that key ingredients to good liturgy are a welcoming community, celebrating in one's language, good music, and engaging homilies. Strategies connecting young adults with liturgy and worship include the following:

- Encourage homilists to address a wide range of life's issues.

- Invite young adults to be liturgical ministers, and provide the necessary training.

- Be flexible and respect their time availability when developing criteria for participation in liturgical ministries.

- Remember the needs and life experiences of young adults when preparing prayers.

- Extend a special invitation to men and women in their late teens, twenties, and thirties to participate in prayer and reflection groups.

- Remember that worship in most parishes is intergenerational, gathering in single persons, students, and married couples with or without children.

PASTORAL CARE

The Church has many opportunities to provide young adults with pastoral care. At these times, it is important to be sensitive to their issues and to respond pastorally. The following are some of the strategies for pastoral care with young adults:

- Train people who provide pastoral care and counseling in parishes, on campuses, in the military, or within organizations and movements to be aware of the developmental tasks of young adults.

- Form a peer-counseling or support group.

- Provide a means of communication so young adults who are sick at home or in the hospital can be visited by someone from the parish and can receive the sacraments.

- Consider providing, in cooperation with trained professionals, intervention and prevention programs for young adults at risk for drug and sexual abuse.

GOAL THREE: CONNECTING YOUNG ADULTS WITH THE MISSION OF THE CHURCH IN THE WORLD

To invite young adults, through healthy relationships, work, and studies, to embrace the mission of Christ to promote the building of the kingdom of God in the world today, thereby bringing about the transformation of society.

Objectives

Forming a Christian Conscience: To help young adults form their conscience based on the Gospel and on the Church's moral and social teachings.

Educating and Working for Justice: To provide educational and service opportunities for young adults to practice the gospel values of justice and peace and to care for the less fortunate in the workplace, at home, and in the local community.

Developing Leaders for the Present and the Future: To invite, train, support, and mentor young adults to be leaders in society and church life.

Strategies to Implement Goal Three
FORMING A CHRISTIAN CONSCIENCE

In the Post-Synodal Apostolic Exhortation on the Laity, *Christifideles Laici*, John Paul II speaks of the role of the laity as the evangelizers of society through the home and work. Faith communities

have a responsibility to prepare and support the laity in this task. In our meetings with young adults, we heard their desire to learn more about the Church in order to make sound moral decisions. Conscience formation is one of the most important aspects in ministry today. Some strategies for helping young adults to develop a Christian conscience include the following:

- Offer adult religious education programs that connect contemporary life issues to the teachings and traditions of the Church.

- Provide seminars and discussion groups to examine the relationship of faith to work, including ethics in the workplace. These can take the form of a breakfast with a speaker from the local business community or university or as a lunch presentation for downtown churches.

- Make use of homilies and sacramental celebrations, where appropriate, to incorporate a discussion of the role of the laity as evangelizers of society.

- Support and facilitate scripture study groups and small groups for married couples.

- Support the formation of ongoing, intergenerational small faith communities.

EDUCATING AND WORKING FOR JUSTICE

Throughout our history, we as Catholics have been driven by a mission to care for the least among us. In 1991, we celebrated the one hundredth anniversary of the encyclical *Rerum Novarum*, a landmark document on social justice and the workplace. This ministry of justice and service is both action on behalf of the poor and education. Programs, homilies, and retreats must educate people to the demands of the Gospel toward our neighbor. Some suggestions for action include the following:

- Motivate young adults, through catechesis, preaching, and music, to be just and to work for peace in their relationships with others, especially in their jobs and in the community.

- Invite young adults to be members of the parish or campus social justice committees or other social action organizations.

- Identify opportunities for immersion experiences during academic breaks or vacations.

- Invite young adults individually, through the workplace or through the church community, to donate services to social service agencies.

DEVELOPING LEADERS FOR THE PRESENT AND THE FUTURE

A key way to form leaders for the present and the future, for both society and the Church, is through mentoring relationships. Mentoring is a significant way in which we equip young adults with the values, beliefs, ideas, and learning necessary to be mature Christians. Young adults can benefit from mentoring relationships connected with their career and job, especially when we share the values and wisdom that spring from our belief in the Gospel. To develop mentoring relationships, include the following:

- Establish a committee to connect older and younger adults in like professions in mentoring relationships.

- Reinforce the leadership role that each Christian is asked to undertake as a citizen through preaching and catechetical opportunities.

For me, I can get through the tough times of life better when I know that there are people I can go to for support or just to talk.

Cynthia Standt, Salem, Ohio

- Form discussion, support, or prayer groups for those in like professions and trades.

- Ask young adults to be mentors for high school youth, especially youth in confirmation programs and those from different ethnic groups, including immigrants who need to learn how to succeed in a new and different culture.

GOAL FOUR: CONNECTING YOUNG ADULTS WITH A PEER COMMUNITY

To help young adults develop relationships with peers who share similar values and beliefs which nurture and strengthen their faith, thereby creating communities of support.

Objectives

Forming Faith Communities of Peers: To provide opportunities for young adults to find among their peers the necessary support and encouragement as they journey through life and fulfill their mission to the world.

Developing Peer Leadership: To help young adults become leaders, not only among their peers but also within the larger community.

Identifying a Young Adult Team: To urge each parish, movement, organization, and campus to identify a team to advocate and respond to the needs of young adults.

Strategies to Implement Goal Four

FORMING FAITH COMMUNITIES OF PEERS

Young adults express a need for support from and relationships with others who are their own age or are in similar situations. We urge pastors and other church leaders to develop specific opportunities for young adults to be together. While it will be helpful to have someone from the parish or campus staff as a point of contact, young adults should be the organizers and leaders of these efforts. We know from experience that they are effective ministers, especially among their peers.

Activities for Single Young Adults

Today, a sizable number of men and women remain single during their late teens, twenties, and thirties. It is important for the Church to have an appropriate ministry with single Catholics. Many single people speak of feeling left out of parish life when the focus is solely on families. Single young adults can be a rich resource of time and talent for the local faith community. Suggested strategies for the Church's ministry with single men and women include the following:

• Invite single men and women to participate in the parish's liturgical, catechetical, social justice, and youth ministries.

• Allow single young adults to plan social and spiritual activities for people in similar life situations. Some singles may wish to form a small Christian community for prayer, Scripture study, and community service.

• Plan a retreat or discussion group with topics of interest to single people such as dating, sexuality, loneliness, careers, and volunteerism. The content should view these issues through the "lens" of faith and provide adequate time for discussion and sharing of personal stories.

• Discuss with the organizations and ministries of the parish how they can welcome and involve single men and women in their activities.

Programs to Assist Newly Married

Once the wedding is over and the honeymoon is a wonderful memory, the real work of marriage begins. The faith community should continue the hospitality and welcome offered during the marriage preparation period, so the couple remains part of the local church. In fact, we can describe Christian marriage preparation as "a journey of faith that does not end with the celebration of marriage but continues throughout life."[41] Follow-up ministry with newly married couples develops what was begun in marriage preparation.[42] Suggestions for follow-up include the following:

• Send anniversary cards, hold a newly married couples support group in the parish, or host an anniversary supper for couples married in the past year. This shows an ongoing concern for the couples and helps to keep them connected during the early years of marriage, when the divorce rate is highest.

- Consider extending the mentoring process for engaged couples through the first year of marriage, especially if the couples remain in the area.

- Invite married couples to participate in a parish ministry or activity.

- Be sensitive to time constraints. Do not automatically exclude young couples who frequently enjoy ministering in the parish.

- Sponsor discussion or educational groups to consider issues relating to maintaining a marriage. Some themes might include changing relationships in the families of origin, managing a household, finances, communication, disagreements, and understanding of the theology of marriage.

- Invite those celebrating anniversaries to renew their marriage vows at special Sunday liturgies during the year.

- Inform their new parish when newly married couples move from the parish.

- Provide couples who are struggling in their marriages with information about marriage counseling.

- Create educational, spiritual, and social opportunities where young married couples can be with each other. This can include the formation of small Christian communities.

Encouragement for Families with Young Children

Young adults who are starting a family are entering a world that is quite unfamiliar to them. Finding support and affirmation from family, friends, and the church community can enable them to adjust to these new experiences, which are both joyful and stressful. In this manner, the Church supports parents as the primary evangelizers and educators of their children. Some of the ways to minister to families with young children include the following:

- Develop a support group for parents of young children. Identify times and places that are convenient and accessible. Provide the opportunity for child care during activities and programs.

- Invite experienced parents to mentor young couples who are having their first child. This can be especially helpful for those without family in the area.

- Design a retreat for new parents, centered on the gift of life.

- Identify liturgical opportunities throughout the year to celebrate parenthood and families, for example, Baptism of the Lord (January), Holy Family Sunday (December).

- Develop a special prayer booklet with prayers and family-centered home activities for meal times and evenings.

DEVELOPING PEER LEADERSHIP

If the Church is to continue to regenerate and renew its members, the training of young adults is key. Young men and women already provide valuable service in the Church. Parishes and campuses should provide them with leadership training, especially for core members of the young adult commission and parish staff.

Young adults recognize that training is central to competency. They have been trained for their job, profession, or trade. They continuously attend workshops and seminars to increase their knowledge and skills. They expect to be managed with competence and treated with respect and dignity. For the growth of the Church, continuing education is also necessary. Young adults who volunteer time for parish ministry will need to learn more about the Church and to develop the necessary ministerial skills. To develop peer leadership, include the following strategies:

- Provide leadership training for young adults in peer ministry. These can be weekend and/or evening programs. They can be sponsored by the diocese or campus or held in conjunction with a lay ministry formation program.

- Use adult education principles in peer leadership development.

- Choose topics for training programs such as starting a ministry, building core teams, planning activities, and working with volunteers. Also, familiarize young adult leaders with the teachings and traditions of the Church.

- Develop an informational program for the pastoral staff, leadership team, and pastoral

> What does the Church and the pope expect of the young people . . . ? That you confess Jesus Christ. And that you learn to proclaim all that the message of Christ contains for the true liberation and genuine progress of humanity. This is what Christ expects of you. This is what the Church looks for in you.
>
> World Youth Day Vigil at Luneta Park, January 14, 1995

council on ministering with young adults. Topics can include the faith and life development of young adults and principles for ministry with young adults.

IDENTIFYING A YOUNG ADULT TEAM

In this plan, we suggest that each parish, organization, and campus, where possible, identify a young adult team and/or a contact person. This team is the link between the Church and the local young adult community. The team advocates for the needs of young adults and works with someone on the staff as a point of reference. The team also can plan and implement activities and programs directed to the young adult community. The team should be given adequate training and be willing to collaborate with those responsible for the various ministries of the community. Young adult team leaders may wish to identify one contact person as a liaison with the diocese and other young adult efforts.

PART

The Campus, the Diocese, and Catholic Organizations

FOUR

CAMPUS MINISTRY CENTERS

Campus ministry is first and foremost ministry in and with the academic community—with those involved in teaching and learning. Few would disagree that the "college years are a very significant time" for young adults.[43] As we said in our *Letter to College Students*, in these years students greatly expand both their knowledge and their skills. They also make some very important decisions about vocation, relationships, and career. Therefore, it is only appropri-

ate that the Church seeks to be a partner with the college or university in the cognitive and moral development of young adults.

Campus ministry is essentially ministry in higher education. It has an important role in helping students to assess the knowledge they are acquiring through the eyes of faith and to discern how they will use that knowledge in their profession. Because these Catholics are in the process of occupying leadership roles in society, theological reflection and moral formation are key.

While similar in many respects, campus ministry centers differ from parishes in a number of ways. The vast majority of people involved in campus

43

ministry are young adults, while parishes are typically intergenerational communities. Campus ministry centers usually do not have the large number of families with school-aged children that some parishes have. However, some ministries to higher education are organized as parishes whose parishioners may or may not be affiliated with the university or college.

> *There are many specific ways that you can minister on campus to create a climate of hope and a community of welcome. Begin by inviting your friends and neighbors to join you at Sunday Mass....*
>
> Letter to College Students from the
> U.S. Catholic Bishops, 1995, p. 3.

While campus ministry involves young adults, it is separate and distinct from young adult ministry. In the years since *Empowered by the Spirit*, our 1985 pastoral letter on campus ministry, many campus ministries have become creative centers of liturgy, community outreach, and spiritual development. In that pastoral letter, we identified "six ways in which the Church on campus can be a faithful witness to the message of the Gospel: forming the faith community, appropriating the faith, forming the Christian conscience, educating for justice, facilitating personal development, and developing leaders for the future."[44] We have used these six actions as the basis for the objectives we have set forth in this plan of action.

Many students have participated in these creative and empowering campus ministry experiences. This environment has allowed them to use their talents and to develop leadership skills that have helped them appreciate not only their giftedness but also the role that they can play in building faith communities. A major transition occurs when these young adults leave campus and look to be welcomed into church life at the parish level. Many tell us of experiences where they were not encouraged or invited to participate. Sometimes, their initiative is discounted and they are ignored. They feel frustrated and left out, leading them, at times, to seek a more welcoming community.

Campus ministry centers can help with this transition. They can collaborate with dioceses and parishes to help college students return to parish life. An explicit strategy to assist with this move needs to be developed by each campus center and diocese. This strategy should include equipping young adults for the transition, providing suggestions for engaging parish leaders, and providing lists to students of young adult friendly parishes. Young adults and the leadership of the parish, both ordained and lay, can develop specific initiatives to welcome returning students and recent graduates.

One specific strategy is to conduct workshops, using graduates who have successfully transitioned to a parish. A typical workshop can include community building activities and opportunities to identify specific needs and discuss solutions. The personal witness of young adults is key. Active and successful young adult ministry programs can be promoted and profiled. Campuses also may wish to keep a list of diocesan young adult coordinators because on any one campus, Catholic students will be from many different dioceses.

Other strategies to assist young adults returning from campus life to parish life include the following:

- Extend parish hospitality by including materials on young adult ministry activities in the welcome packets.

- List the name of a young adult contact person in the parish bulletin.

- Extend a special verbal invitation to young adults to participate in existing programs and ministries.

- Identify young adults who move into the parish, and contact them about participation in parish ministries.

- Allow young adults to have the same access to parish facilities that is extended to other parish groups.

> When I returned home from college, I wanted to be part of something and to be around others who like me had a deep faith. Instead, I felt alone and isolated; nobody made me feel welcome. . . .
>
> Nariman Ayyad, North Bellmore, N.Y.

DIOCESAN STRATEGIES

The diocese has a unique role to play in ministry with young adults. Our Church is more alive when all of our church agencies and institutions work together toward a common goal. In this way, we can give our people many opportunities to experience God's grace and the Church's care for them. Pastors, campus ministers, and leaders of organizations will look to the diocese for support and resources in developing ministry with young adults.

The diocese can be more effective than the parish or campus center in undertaking certain initiatives. The diocesan office can draw together young adults throughout the city or region for conferences, can provide worship experiences leading to a greater awareness of the universality of the Church, and can promote a young adult perspective within diocesan offices, parishes, campuses, and other diocesan-wide organizations.

Each diocese can assess its own needs regarding this ministry and can develop appropriate responses. No one model will be useful to every diocese in this country, but we can identify several proven approaches based on current practice and experience.

One approach is to establish a young adult commission that mirrors the different cultural, ethnic, educational, vocational, social, and economic spiritual realities of the diocese or region. Members might include young adults from the various regions, vicariates, and ethnic groups; parish leaders and young adult contacts; and representatives from campuses within the diocese and from Catholic movements and organizations. One responsibility of the young adult commission can be to plan, coordinate, and implement the diocesan or regional activities.

FUNCTIONS OF A DIOCESAN-WIDE MINISTRY WITH YOUNG ADULTS

Dioceses can assist parish and campus leaders in several ways:

- Provide parishes and campuses with resources on young adulthood and ministry with young adults, especially those that highlight the developmental tasks and different ethnic groups of the diocese.

- Assist parishes and campuses with implementing this pastoral plan by developing guidelines and resources.

- Provide parish and campus leadership and young adult team members with training and leadership development appropriate for each of the cultures that make up the local Church.

- Support parish and campus efforts for ministry with young adults through personal presence.

- Advocate for ministry with young adults, supporting parish and campus young adult contacts and other diocesan staff who work with young adults.

- Advocate that young adults from all ethnic groups be invited to become members of diocesan committees and commissions. Appoint several young adults to the diocesan pastoral council or young adult priests to the diocesan priests' council.

- Sponsor activities that bring young adults together such as conferences, regional educational opportunities, yearly worship experiences, and social activities. In those dioceses with different ethnic populations, have conferences that promote a significant dialogue among young people from different cultures.

COLLABORATION AMONG DIOCESAN OFFICES

If a diocese wishes to undertake a comprehensive and effective ministry to and with young adults, collaboration and coordination among diocesan offices become important. Whether the diocese chooses to identify an office for young adults or identify a staff person as a contact or facilitator for this ministry, collaboration is essential. Together, diocesan offices can assist and connect parishes and campuses in ways that are otherwise not possible for a single parish, campus ministry center, or military chaplaincy. When diocesan offices collaborate, they have the ability to cross cultural and economic lines and manifest the universality and catholicity of the Church.

We know that ministry to and with young adults is now undertaken by several offices within the diocese including Religious Education and Lay Formation (adult catechesis and spritual formation); Family Life (marriage preparation, ministry to the newly married); offices for different ethnic ministries (African American, Asian American, and Hispanic); Social Action (Christian service and education for justice); Liturgy (RCIA, liturgical ministries); Campus Ministry (pastoral life on college/university campuses); Youth Ministry (many parish youth ministers are young adults); and the Tribunal and Chancery (many people seeking annulments and dispensations are young adults). Some dioceses have separate young adult offices while others have linked their outreach to young adults with the Youth Ministry office in

recent years. Some dioceses have Pastoral Juvenil Hispana offices, which focus on single Hispanic young adults. However the local Church is organized, remember that ministry with young adults is separate and distinct from adolescent ministry and is primarily a ministry to and with adults.

COLLABORATION WITH THE MILITARY

The United States military contains the single largest group of young adult Catholics in this country. Because of this, we suggest that diocesan and parish leaders coordinate efforts and collaborate with the military chaplain's office at the local base, whenever appropriate. Both the diocese and the chaplain's office have access to resources that can be shared thereby enriching the faith lives of young adults.

REGIONALIZATION

Currently, regional young adult ministry is an effective and successful approach in many dioceses. Regionalization is particularly effective where there are many smaller parishes or campuses in the same area or where the geographic size or population of the diocese lends itself to smaller groupings. Collaborating parishes, campus ministry centers, and dioceses can pool and share resources that may be unavailable to a single parish, campus ministry center, or diocese.

CATHOLIC ORGANIZATIONS AND MOVEMENTS

The Church is blessed with many Catholic organizations and movements. They provide a special ministry to young adults, furthering their spiritual growth and nurturing a willingness to be of   service to humankind. Many of these organizations and movements were originally founded by young adults. Still today, they can benefit from the energy and vitality.

Catholic organizations and movements can provide young adults with a community, an association with a particular charism, and a sense of service and mission. Thus, these organizations and movements bear the most fruit where they are integrated into the local Church under the leadership of the bishop and/or the universal Church under the leadership of the Holy Father.

We ask our Catholic organizations and movements to join us in connecting young adults with the Church. We ask that they welcome young adults and allow them

adequate opportunities to participate and lead. As in the parish and on campus, organizations and movements will be effective in attracting young adults if they consider the pastoral, spiritual, and physical needs of these young men and women. An intergenerational membership is rich in wisdom and talent, especially when all members feel that their concerns are addressed.

I wish every Church would take into account what young adults say and give us a chance to show what we can do.

Veronica Ortega, Texas

PART

Implementation of the Pastoral Plan

FIVE

GETTING STARTED

The value of any plan depends on the ability of the local community—a diocese, parish, campus, military chaplaincy or organization—to implement its strategies. This section of the pastoral plan will help pastoral planners begin the implementation process. Throughout the implementation, continue to pray for wisdom, understanding, and guidance from the Holy Spirit. Below are ten steps to start your outreach and ministry.

1. *Form a core team to undertake the necessary assessment, planning, and implementation.* This can be comprised of young adults who have already demonstrated some interest or leadership in the parish or campus or of young adults known to a staff member. Other members on the core team may be from the parish or campus pastoral council, professional staff, and interested adults and young adults. Depending on the situation, an already existing group might be asked to undertake the necessary assessment, planning, and implementation. If the local Church has young adults from different ethnic and cultural groups, consult with them to identify

the best approaches for evangelization and ministry. There should be at least two or three people from each significant ethnic group on the core team. This is even more important where there are different language groups or great diversity in the same church community. Once the core team has been formed, they should study this plan of action. It is also necessary to provide ongoing education and formation for the core team, staff, and other ministry leaders.

2. *Assess the situation in your local community.* Consider using the following questions to assess the present situation of young adults—both single and married—in church life. What does the community know about young adults? How do young adults perceive the local church community? How easy is it for young adults and newcomers to get involved? How sensitive and responsive is the community to the needs of young adults, especially those who are alienated and unchurched or those from various ethnic groups? How do the issues we have discussed relate to the lives of young adults? How does the preaching stimulate and challenge them to deeper faith and action? Use the principles listed in this plan to develop further assessment questions.

3. *Complete an inventory of what is already taking place.* Identify what programs exist in the community specifically for young adults and those where young adults are part of a larger church ministry or program. Determine how many young adults are presently involved in these programs, ministries, and apostolates. Try to determine how many young adults live within the community but do not participate. Where possible, find out how old they are, whether they are single, married, engaged, divorced, or single again. Try to assess why young adults participate in or are absent from church life.

4. *Educate and provide formation.* Gather the diocesan, parish and/or campus leadership to study this plan of action. Identify ways in which the local Church can be more accessible to young adults. Involve the participation of several young adults from the ethnic group(s) within the community. Arrange for training in leadership and small-group skills. For assistance, contact the diocesan office responsible for young adults.

5. *Improve involvement, participation, and integration.* Determine how the diocese, parish, or campus invites young adults to be involved in current programs, ministries, and apostolates. Develop a realistic strategy by identifying steps to improve the outreach to young adults. Use the four goals of this plan and the input of young adults; they will know what works best for their age group.

6. *Invite and welcome.* Develop a response that is based on personal outreach to those who are not currently involved, to the unchurched, or to those who have left the Church.

7. *Offer new activities, organizations, and programs.* Once the leadership of the community has assessed the situation of young adults, build on current opportunities and organize new activities, organizations, and programs. Use the goals, objectives, and

suggested strategies as starting points for your outreach and ministry.

8. *Identify peer initiatives and activities*. At times, it may be necessary to create similar but separate programs for young adults. Older adults may not always be comfortable working with young adults, and some activities are better accomplished within the peer group. Understand that the mobility and the schedules of young adults demand more flexibility and occasional programming. They may not be able to commit themselves to weekly or multiple-session programs, but they can participate in single-session activities and individual programs.

9. *Establish a multi-year implementation plan*. Set up a three-year implementation plan with realistic and achievable objectives based on the four goals of this plan. Identify specific

ways to measure success. Evaluate your efforts repeatedly and consistently. Discuss funding requirements with parish and diocesan leadership.

10. *Keep the vision*. Keep the vision of young adult ministry in the forefront and let it guide your work. When initiatives do not work as planned, critique them, but do not give up on your dream. Identify people locally and nationally to be your mentors and support. Contact the national organizations whose mission it is to continue effective outreach and ministry with young adults.

By investing in young adults today, the Church will yield much in the future in the forms of stewardship, leadership, and vocations. Further, young adults' investment in the Church will be one hundred fold because of their talents, abilities, education and desire to serve.

Kris Egan, Iowa

FINAL PRAYER

Gracious and Loving God,

Help these young men and women to be a light for all the world to see,
in all the places they live and work.

Let their light shine for all peoples:
for their families,
for their church communities,
for their cultures and societies,
for the economic and political systems,
for the whole world.

Coming into the room where the disciples were gathered after the resurrection,
"Jesus, your son, said: Peace be with you!" (Jn 20:21).

Make these men and women bearers of Christ's peace.

Teach them the meaning of what was said on the mountain:
"Blessed are the peacemakers,
for they shall be called sons and daughters of God" (cf. Mt 5:9).

Send them, Father, as you sent your son:
to free their brothers and sisters from fear and sin.

We ask this of you, in Christ's name. Amen.

Adapted from the Papal Homily for WYD 1995, Manila

RESOURCES

In addition to the resources mentioned throughout this document and in the notes, the following are suggested.

Archdiocese of Omaha. *A Pastoral Plan for Young Adult Ministry*. Omaha, Neb.: KP Printing, 1994. A plan of action for ministering to the young adults of the archdiocese developed by the Young Adult Advisory Board.

Bagley, Rev. Ron, CJM (ed). *Young Adult Ministry: A Book of Readings*. Naugatuck, Conn.: Center for Ministry Development, 1987. A collection of essays on three basic themes: foundations for young adult ministry, perspectives on young adults, and directions for ministry.

Fowler, James. *Becoming Adult, Becoming Christian: Adult Development and Christian Faith*. San Francisco: Harper and Row, 1984.

Gallup International Institute. *The Religious Life of Young Americans*. A compendium of surveys on the spiritual beliefs and practices of teenagers and young adults.

Gribbon, Robert. *Developing Faith in Young Adults: Effective Ministry with 18-35 Year Olds*. Washington, D.C.: The Alban Institute, 1990.

Muto, Susan. *Celebrating the Single Life*. New York: Doubleday & Company, Inc., 1982. Explores the joys of being single, the spirituality of singles in the Church, service to others as a single person, and friendships.

National Catholic Young Adult Ministry Association. *A Blueprint for Young Adult Ministry*. Washington, D.C.: National Catholic Young Adult Ministry Association, 1994. A short reflection discussing what young adult ministry is and the foundational and operational principles for ministry with young adults.

National Conference of Catholic Bishops. *Follow the Way of Love*. Washington, D.C.: United States Catholic Conference, 1994. Bishops' pastoral message to married couples and families.

O'Brien, Sr. Margaret. *Discovering Your Light: Common Journey of Young Adults*. Mineola, N.Y.: Resurrection Press, Ltd., 1991. A workbook for men and women in their twenties and thirties that can be used as a private journal or in small faith-sharing groups.

Roof, Wade Clark. *A Generation of Seekers*. San Francisco: Harper, 1993. A book addressing the baby boomer generation's search for spirituality.

United States Catholic Conference. *Empowered by the Spirit*. Washington, D.C.: United States Catholic Conference, 1985. This is the U.S. bishops' pastoral plan for ministry on the campus.

_____. *Family Perspective in Church and Society*. Washington, D.C.: United States Catholic Conference, 1987.

_____. *Who Are My Sisters and Brothers? Reflections on Understanding and Welcoming Immigrants and Refugees*. Washington, D.C.: United States Catholic Conference, 1996.